Prayers for those experiencing Spiritual Affliction

compiled
by
Bishop Julian Porteous

All booklets are published thanks to the generous support of the members of the Catholic Truth Society

CATHOLIC TRUTH SOCIETY
PUBLISHERS TO THE HOLY SEE

Contents

 First published 2012 by The Incorporated Catholic Truth Society 40-46 Harleyford Road, London SE11 5AY Tel: 020 7640 0042 Fax: 020 7640 0046.

ISBN 978 1 86082 792 1

Introduction

This small booklet offers the believer some resources of prayer when confronted with the experience of spiritual affliction. People can experience various types of spiritual affliction and as they turn to the Church to ask for assistance our Catholic tradition can offer prayers that they can use to assist them in resisting evil and finding comfort and healing. These prayers offer a means to seek the mercy of God coming to their aid. The booklet draws on the spiritual tradition of the Church in offering a variety of prayers. Different prayers will be suited for different needs and situations.

The struggle with the powers of evil is part of the experience of every human being. While human beings have a natural orientation towards the good we find ourselves confronting evil in various ways.

We all experience temptation in various ways, and daily life is a struggle against falling into sin. The use of the sacraments, especially the Sacraments of Reconciliation and Holy Communion, and the practice of prayer and other spiritual exercises are a source of spiritual strengthening against temptation.

Some people can come under the influence of the powers of evil in more explicit ways. Some find themselves caught in forms of *oppression*. If we describe temptation as an inclination coming from without, oppression is something whereby a person senses that they are in the grip of forces that are quite overwhelming. This is the case where we experience a very strong drive to do something that we know is damaging to ourselves or to others. It can be drug taking, binge drinking, gambling, stealing or pornography. This is the area of addictions. A person here senses the power of an attraction to do something that is damaging to themselves and which is quite overwhelming. There is the feeling that the addiction is too strong to resist. Our freedom to decide is diminished. This attraction is oppressive. We can find that giving in to the craving only makes it more difficult to resist next time. We can find that we have become trapped. This is the lot of the drug addict, the alcoholic, the gambler.

When we turn to the gospel of St. Mark we note that the first miracle recorded is that of Jesus being confronted by and then casting out a demon in the synagogue (see *Mk* 1:21-28). What is of interest is that the demon initiates the confrontation by calling out, "What do you want with us Jesus of Nazareth? Have you come to destroy us?" It is as though evil is threatened by the presence of Jesus. It suggests that this is the battle that is about to be waged. God is going to challenge the free reign that evil has had over the lives of people.

The gospels record a number of instances of such a confrontation. The mentality of the time readily ascribed to demons forms of oppression that afflicted people. Today we might be more circumspect in attributing some afflictions to the influence of demons, explaining such conditions in psychological terms. However, as we have seen already we cannot eliminate the possibility of the influence and power of demonic forces coupled with something that may also have a psychological cause.

Obsessions like gambling, pornography and substance abuse are destructive of human character and have a spiritual dimension as well as physical and psychological dimensions. People can experience being assailed by forms of darkness that can be overwhelming – such as fears of various kinds, memories of rejection or injustice, depression, a sense of worthlessness. These are very real and can be quite debilitating. Some can be helped by psychology and medication, but the person suffers a real debilitating power which is a burden for their lives. Added to these experiences are others that could be termed torments of the soul – for instance an enduring bitterness, an irrational jealousy. These are the "demons" that infest our lives. In our common speech we speak about "facing our demons."

Such experiences mean that the person is not totally free. The person may be substantially burdened and in the grip of forces over which they have little or no control.

Points of entry for the power of evil to gain influence over our lives can be from such experiences as trauma or an area where we have been wounded. It can be due to habitual sin of a serious kind where a person has begun to lose control over behaviour. It can be the result of involvement in the occult where a person seeking power through other than divine influences allows demonic entry. Or it can have an origin in past generations where there have been sinful patterns or curses from our ancestry.

Satan is a defeated enemy, but he is still able to conduct "guerrilla warfare" on humanity. There are many ways in which the devil is able to gain a damaging hold in people's lives.

The first is when sin, or more importantly, habits of sin, become a feature of a person's life. This gives Satan a particular foothold. He is able to expand the dimensions of this sin and increase its detrimental effect. Various forms of apostasy, or rejection of God, open the door for the presence of the powers of darkness. Wilful rejection of the Church and its teaching makes a person susceptible to the influence of demonic forces. In such an instance a person has removed himself from the protection of the Church.

Then too, increased interest these days in other religions such as Buddhism, Hinduism, or various pagan religions can lead people outside the protection of the Christian faith. The adopting of various practices emerging from these non-Christian sources – like Yoga and Reiki – is fraught with danger. Even a Christian delving into these practices can be spiritually affected without realising it.

Dabbling in the occult, which is quite widespread, is a more immediate opportunity for demonic activity. Any form of divinisation – séances, fortune telling, Ouija boards, tarot cards – is a sin against faith and invites in evil spirits. Even "white magic" – Wicca, for instance – sought as a source of healing can lead to deception and the influence of demons.

The general rise of interest in the New Age has become a significant source for people coming under the influence of the powers of darkness. Even what may appear innocuous can become the doorway to entry into a dark and dangerous world.

As well as these potential sources for demonic activity in a person, the general state of a person's soul can be fertile ground for evil spirits. If a person is engaged in sexual perversions, pornography, or the use of drugs, the door is opened to the powers of darkness.

Some people have very fragile personalities and may carry serious defects of character as a result of upbringing or particular experiences. Serious insecurities that manifest themselves in depression or low self-esteem can provide avenues for demonic presence.

It is also important to mention that people well advanced in the Christian life can become subject to intense demonic attack. The Book of Job recounts the story of a just man who is tested to the extreme. Many saints attest to the darkest of intense personal struggles, for example St Antony of Egypt, St John Vianney, St Pio of Pictrelcina.

Finally, mention needs to be made of specific engagement with satanic rites. There are indications that there is a rise in this sort of activity and a morbid fascination with dark rituals. This, of course, is a most dangerous activity and will have deep and lasting consequences.

Every person has an individual struggle with Satan. The Sacraments of Baptism and Confirmation are the means by which we become Children of God. We belong to God and this identity should not be underestimated in the spiritual struggle. We are Children of Light – as the Baptismal Rite declares – and do not belong to the powers of darkness. In these sacraments we receive the Holy Spirit, who is the agent of God's sanctifying presence within us – the "mark of God's ownership" (*Ep* 1:13).

In the Rite of Baptism we formally reject Satan and "all his empty works and promises." In the three-fold formula we formally renounce evil and proclaim our intention to be "Children of the Light."

The Christian still must contend daily with temptation to sin. The Church has traditionally urged every believer to live in Christ and use prayer, fasting and the sacramental life - particularly the Rite of Penance - as ordinary means to resist temptation and grow in holiness.

It is important to recognise that sin which is not brought to the Sacrament of Penance can induce spiritual weakness and susceptibility to demonic activity. Every Catholic should take seriously the need for regular Confession as a means of being strengthened to resist temptation. The Confessional is also the place where a person struggling with particular temptations can receive not only forgiveness for failures, but the grace to be stronger in maintaining the spiritual struggle. The confessor can also assist the person with sound spiritual advice.

The Christian tradition regularly utilises the practice of invoking the mercy of God. The prayer of the publican – "Lord, be merciful to me a sinner" (*Lk* 18:9-14) – is the basis for many practices in liturgy and devotion. At each Mass we use the three-fold formula: "Lord have mercy, Christ have mercy, Lord have mercy." This prayer, said in a heart-felt manner, is heard. The Christian East has adopted the "Jesus Prayer" – "Lord Jesus Christ, Son of the living God, be merciful to me a sinner" – as the ground for developing the spiritual life. This prayer can be a powerful means of relying upon the saving action of God to assist us in overcoming sin and resisting temptation.

May this booklet be a source of spiritual comfort and a means of obtaining grace and protection from God.

Bishop Julian Porteous
Auxiliary Bishop of Sydney
27 June 2011

Renewal of Baptismal Promises

A person struggling against the powers of evil can use their Baptismal Promises as a sign of their desire to give their lives completely to Jesus Christ, as Lord and Saviour. Said with faith and fervour the Baptismal Promises confirm our desire to live wholly under the guidance and protection of God.

Q. Do you reject sin so as to live in the freedom of God's children?

A. I do.

Q. Do you reject the glamour of evil and refuse to be mastered by sin?

A. I do.

Q. Do you reject Satan, Father of Sin, and Prince of Darkness?

A. I do.

Q. Do you believe in God, the Father almighty, Creator of Heaven and earth?

A. I do.

Q. Do you believe in Jesus Christ, his only Son, our Lord, who was born of the Virgin Mary, was crucified, died, and was buried, rose from the dead, and is now seated at the right hand of the Father?

A. I do.

Q. Do you believe in the Holy Spirit, the holy Catholic Church, the communion of Saints, the forgiveness of sins, the resurrection of the body, and life everlasting?

A. I do.

The Lord's Prayer

The great prayer that the Lord taught us concluding with the words, "deliver us from evil," should be said.

Our Father who art in Heaven, hallowed be Thy name; Thy kingdom come, Thy will be done on earth as it is in Heaven. Give us this day our daily bread, and forgive us our trespasses, as we forgive those who trespass against us; and lead us not into temptation, but deliver us from evil. Amen.

The Psalms

A number of the psalms are very suitable as prayers of deliverance. Psalm 90(91) is particularly appropriate. Other psalms include 3, 10(11), 12(13), 21(22), 30(31), 34(35), 53(54), 67(68), and 69(70). The psalm number given is from the Greek Septuagint which is used in Christian liturgies and the number in parentheses is the Hebrew numbering which is found in most Bibles.

Texts from the Gospels

Texts of Holy Scripture can be read in association with prayers for deliverance. The Rite of Exorcism identifies the following Gospel readings:

Matthew 4:1-11	The Temptation of Jesus
Mark 1:21-28	The Cure of the Demoniac
Mark 16:15-18	The Commissioning of the Eleven
Luke 10:17-20	The Return of the Seventy-two
Luke 11:14-24	Jesus and Beelzebul
John 1:1-14	The Prologue

Anima Christi

This ancient prayer is used by St Ignatius of Loyola in his Spiritual Exercises. It has an earlier origin and reflects a solid Eucharistic theology and draws on the devotion to the Five Wounds.

Soul of Christ, sanctify me.
Body of Christ, save me.
Blood of Christ, inebriate me.
Water from the side of Christ, wash me.
Passion of Christ, strengthen me.
O good Jesus, hear me.
Within Thy wounds hide me.
Separated from Thee let me never be.
From the malicious enemy defend me.
In the hour of my death call me

And bid me come unto Thee.
That I may praise Thee
with Thy saints and with Thy angels
Forever and ever. Amen.

Prayers invoking the intercession of the Blessed Virgin Mary

The intercession of the Blessed Virgin Mary can be sought through the use of traditional prayers. Some traditional prayers seeking the intercession of the Blessed Virgin Mary are offered below.

Hail Mary

Hail Mary, full of grace, the Lord is with thee. Blessed art thou among women and blessed is the fruit of thy womb, Jesus. Holy Mary, Mother of God, pray for us sinners now and at the hour of our death. Amen.

Memorare

Remember, O most gracious Virgin Mary, that never was it known that anyone who fled to thy protection, implored thy help, or sought thine intercession was left unaided. Inspired by this confidence, I fly unto thee, O Virgin of virgins, my mother; to thee do I come, before thee I stand, sinful and sorrowful. O Mother of the Word Incarnate, despise not my petitions, but in thy mercy hear and answer me. Amen.

Prayer to Our Lady, Queen of the Angels

August Queen of Heaven!
Sovereign Mistress of the angels!
You who from the beginning have received from God
the power and mission to crush the head of Satan.
We humbly beseech you to send your holy Legions,
that under your command and by your power,
they may pursue the evil spirits, encounter them
on every side,
resist their bold attacks and drive them hence into the
abyss of eternal woe.
Amen.

Salve Regina

Hail holy Queen, Mother of mercy; hail our life, our sweetness, and our hope. To thee do we cry, poor banished children of Eve. To thee do we send up our sighs, mourning and weeping in this valley of tears. Turn then, most gracious Advocate, thine eyes of mercy toward us. And after this our exile show unto us the blessed fruit of thy womb, Jesus. O clement, O loving, O sweet Virgin Mary.

V. Pray for us, O Holy Mother of God.

R. That we may be made worthy of the promises of Christ.

Prayer of Pope Leo XIII

The Congregation for the Doctrine of the Faith on 29 September 1985 issued a statement that the exorcism prayers written by Pope Leo should only be used by a priest. However, other parts of his prayers may be used.

O God, our refuge and our strength, look down in mercy on Thy people who cry to Thee: and, by the intercession of the glorious and immaculate Virgin Mary, Mother of God, of Saint Joseph her spouse, of the blessed Apostles Peter and Paul, and of all the Saints, in mercy and goodness hear our prayers for the conversion of sinners, and for the liberty and exaltation of our Holy Mother the Church: through Christ Our Lord. Amen.

Prayer to St Michael the Archangel

Composed by Pope Leo XIII (1878-1903) for the use of all the faithful and was included in the prayers at the end of Mass prior to the reforms of the Second Vatican Council.

Saint Michael, the Archangel, defend us in battle; be our defence against the wickedness and snares of the Devil. May God rebuke him, we humbly pray; and do thou, O Prince of the heavenly host, by the power of God, thrust into Hell Satan and the other evil spirits who prowl about the world for the ruin of souls. Amen.

Guardian Angel Prayer

Angel of God, my guardian dear, to whom God's love commits me here, ever this day be at my side, to light, to guard, to rule and to guide. Amen.

Prayer against Every Evil

Fr Gabriel Amorth, exorcist of the Diocese of Rome, in his book, "An exorcist tells his story," offers a number of prayers of deliverance suitable for lay people to use. The *Prayer against Every Evil, Prayer for Inner Healing* and *Prayer for Deliverance* are included here. These prayers can be recommended to lay people experiencing evil spirits, or can be adapted by priests to pray with such people.

Spirit of our God, Father, Son, and Holy Spirit, Most Holy Trinity, Immaculate Virgin Mary, angels, archangels, and saints of Heaven, descend upon me.

Please purify me, Lord, mould me, fill me with yourself, use me.

Banish from me all the forces of evil, destroy them, vanquish them, so that I can be healthy and do good deeds.

Banish from me all spells, witchcraft, black magic, malefic ties, maledictions, and the evil eye; diabolic infestations, oppressions, possessions; all that is evil and sinful, jealousy, perfidy, envy; physical, psychological, moral, spiritual, diabolical ailments.

Burn all these evils in Hell, that they may never again touch me or any other creature in the entire world.

I command and bid all the powers that molest me – by the power of God all powerful, in the name of Jesus Christ our Saviour, through the intercession of the Immaculate Virgin Mary – to leave me forever, and to be consigned into everlasting Hell, where they will be bound by Saint Michael, Saint Raphael, our guardian angels, and where they will be crushed under the heel of the Immaculate Virgin Mary.

Prayer for Inner Healing

This prayer can be said by or with a person experiencing spiritual burdens associated with demonic influence.

Lord Jesus, you came to heal our wounded and troubled hearts. I beg you to heal the torments that cause anxiety in my heart. I beg you, in a particular way, to heal all who are the cause of sin. I beg you to come into my life and heal me of the psychological harms that struck me in my early years and from the injuries that they caused throughout my life.

Lord Jesus, you know my burdens. I lay them all on your Good Shepherd's heart. I beseech you, by the merits of the great, open wound in your heart, to heal the small wounds that are in mine. Heal the pain of my memories, so that nothing that has happened to me will cause me to remain in pain and anguish, filled with anxiety.

Heal, O Lord, all those wounds that have been the cause of all the evil that is rooted in my life. I want to forgive all those who have offended me. Look to those inner sores that make me unable to forgive. You who came to forgive the afflicted of heart, please, heal my own heart.

Heal, my Lord Jesus, those intimate wounds that cause me physical illness. I offer you my heart, accept it, Lord, purify it and give me the sentiments of your Divine Heart. Help me to be meek and humble.

Heal me, O Lord, from the pain caused by the death of loved ones, which is oppressing me. Grant me to regain peace and joy in the knowledge that you are the Resurrection and the Life. Make me an authentic witness to your resurrection, your victory over sin and death, your living presence among us. Amen.

Prayer for Deliverance

This can be a prayer used as intercession for a person suffering under demonic influence.

My Lord, you are all powerful, you are God, you are Father. We beg you through the intercession and help of the archangels Michael, Raphael and Gabriel for the deliverance of our brothers and sisters who are enslaved by the Evil One. All Saints of Heaven, come to our aid.

[Repeat the invocation ***Free us, O Lord*** after each phrase.]
From anxiety, sadness and obsessions, we beg you.

From hatred, fornication, envy, we beg you.
From thoughts of jealousy, rage and death, we beg you.
From every thought of suicide and abortion we beg you.
From every form of sinful sexuality we beg you.
From every division in our family and every
harmful friendship, we beg you.
From every sort of spell, malefice, witchcraft
and every form of the occult, we beg you.

Lord, you who said, "I leave you peace, my peace I give you," grant that, through the intercession of the Blessed Virgin Mary, we may be liberated from every evil spell and enjoy your peace always. In the name of Christ our Lord. Amen.

A Personal Prayer

This prayer of unknown source is one of many that can be appropriately used by a lay person seeking personal protection from evil spirits. It could be adapted by a priest to apply to a particular person or situation.

Lord, almighty, merciful and omnipotent God,
Father, Son and Holy Spirit, drive out from me
all influence of evil spirits.
Father, in the name of Christ, I plead you to
break any chain that the Devil has on me.
Pour upon me the most precious blood of your Son.
May His immaculate and redeeming blood
break all bonds of my body or mind.

I ask you this through the intercession of the
Most Holy Virgin Mary.
Archangel St Michael, intercede and come to my help.
In the name of Jesus I command all demons that could
have any influence over me, to leave me forever.
By His scourging, His crown of thorns, His cross,
by His blood and Resurrection,
I command all evil spirits to leave me.
By the True God.
By the Holy God.
By God who can do all.
In the name of Jesus, my Saviour and Lord, leave me.
Amen.

Prayer for Protection and Deliverance

This is another prayer of unknown source that can be appropriately used by a lay person seeking personal protection from evil spirits.

Heavenly Father, I praise and thank you for all you have given me. Please cover me with the protective, precious blood of your Son, Jesus Christ, and increase your Holy Spirit in me with His gifts of wisdom, knowledge, understanding, hunger for prayer, guidance and discernment to help me know your will and surrender to it more completely.

Father please heal my negative emotions and any wounds in my heart and spirit. Send the sword of your Holy Spirit to sever and break all spells, curses, hexes, voodoo and all negative genetic, inter-generational and addictive material, past, present or to come, known or unknown, against me, my relationships and family, finances, possessions and ministry.

Father I forgive and I ask forgiveness for my sins and failings and I ask that my whole person, body and mind, heart and will, soul and spirit, memory and emotions, attitudes and values lie cleansed, renewed and protected by the most precious blood of your Son Jesus.

In the name, power, blood and authority of Jesus Christ I bind and break the power and effect in or around me of any and all evil spirits who are trying to harm me in any way and I command these spirits and their companion spirits in the name of the Father, the Son and the Holy Spirit to leave me peacefully and quietly and go immediately and directly to the Eucharistic presence of Jesus Christ in the closest Catholic Church tabernacle, to be disposed of by Jesus and never again return to harm me.

Dear Holy Spirit please fill up any void in me to overflowing with your great love. All this Father I pray in the name of Jesus Christ by the guidance of your Holy Spirit. Immaculate Heart of Mary, spouse of the Holy Spirit, please pray for me and with me. Amen.

Prayer for Protection of Family

Lord Jesus, I ask you to protect my family [mention by name] from sickness, from all harm and from accidents. If any of us has been subjected to any curses, hexes, or spells, I declare these curses, hexes, or spells null and void in the name of Jesus Christ. If any evil spirits have been sent against us, I decommission you in the name of Jesus Christ and I send you to Jesus to deal with as He will. Then, Lord, I ask you to send your holy angels to guard and protect all of us. Amen.

Prayer of Blessing for Buildings

O Father, come and visit our home (shop, office, etc.) and protect us from the lures of the enemy; may your holy angels come to guard our peace and may your blessing remain with us forever in Christ, our Lord. Amen.

Lord Jesus Christ, who said to your apostles, "In whatever home you enter, greet it, saying, 'Peace be in this home,'" let this same peace, we pray, abide in this place. We beseech you to sanctify it by the merits of your glorious death on the Cross. Pour your blessings on it, and make it a place of peace. May salvation enter this abode as it entered the house of Zacchaeus, when you graced it with your presence. Entrust your angels to guard it and banish from it every evil power.

Grant, O God, that all who live (or work) here may please you with their every thought, word, and deed, and so receive from you, when their time comes, the reward of your heavenly home. We ask this through Jesus Christ, our Lord. Amen.

Putting on the Armour of God

This prayer is based on the admonition St. Paul gives in his letter to the Ephesians chapter 6 verses 10-18.

Lord, I place upon my head the helmet of salvation as a protection against all thinking, speaking, seeing, hearing, and feeling, which is not of you.

I place upon my chest the breastplate of righteousness as a protection against all unrighteous thoughts, all fear and anxiety, all sickness and all harm to the body.

I place round my waist the belt of truth that I may be truthful at every level of my being.

I place on my feet the sandals of the gospel of peace that I may be the messenger of your Good News to others.

I take in my left hand the shield of faith with which to quench all the flaming darts of the enemy.

I take in my right hand the sword of the Spirit, which is the word of God, with which to attack the strongholds of the enemy.

St Patrick's Breastplate

St Patrick's Breastplate is contained in the ancient Book of Armagh, from the early ninth century. St Patrick is said to have written this prayer to strengthen himself with God's protection as he prepared to confront and convert Loegaire, high king of Ireland. It is an appropriate prayer for one seeking the protection of God against any evil.

I bind to myself this day,
the strong virtue of the invocation of the Most Holy Trinity,
the faith of the Most Holy Trinity in Unity,
the Creator of the elements.

I bind to myself this day,
the power of the Incarnation of Christ and His baptism,
the power of His Crucifixion with His Burial,
the power of His coming to the sentence of the judgment.

I bind to myself this day,
the power in the love of Seraphim,
in the obedience of Angels,
in the hope of resurrection unto reward,
in the prayers of the Patriarchs,
in the predictions of Prophets,
in the faith of Confessors,
in the purity of Virgins,
in the deeds of Holy Men and Women.

I bind to myself this day,
the power of God to guide me,
the might of God to uphold me,
the wisdom of God to teach me,
the eye of God to watch over me,
the ear of God to hear me,
the word of God to give me speech,
the hand of God to protect me,
the way of God to lie before me,
the shield of God to shelter me,
the host of God to defend me,
against the snares of demons,
against the temptations of vices,
against the lusts of nature,
against every man that meditates injury to me,
whether far or near, alone or with many.

I have invoked all these virtues,
against every hostile, savage power
warring upon my body and soul,
against the enchantments of false prophets,
against the false laws of heresy,
against the deceits of idolatry,
against the spells of women, magicians, and druids,
against all knowledge which binds the soul of man.

Christ protect me this day
against poison, burning, drowning, and wounding,
that I may receive abundant reward.
Christ bc with mc, Christ bcforc mc,
Christ be after me, Christ within me,
Christ below me, Christ above me,
Christ at my right hand, Christ at my left,
Christ in the heart of every man who thinks of me,
Christ in the mouth of every man who speaks to me,
Christ in every eye that sees me,
Christ in every ear that hears me.

I bind to myself this day
the strong faith of the invocation of the Most Holy Trinity,
the faith of the Most Holy Trinity in Unity,
the Creator of the elements,
salvation is the Lord's,
salvation is from Christ,
Thy salvation, O Lord, be with us for ever. Amen.

Litany of the Most Precious Blood

The use of litanies can be most helpful both in personal prayer for protection and in prayer for others. The Litany of the Most Precious Blood is particularly appropriate.

Lord, have mercy.
Christ, have mercy.
Lord, have mercy.

Christ, hear us.
Christ, graciously hear us.

God, the Father of Heaven, *have mercy on us.*
God the Son, Redeemer of the world, *have mercy on us.*
God, the Holy Spirit, *have mercy on us.*
Holy Trinity, One God, *have mercy on us.*

Blood of Christ, only-begotten Son
of the Eternal Father, *save us.*
Blood of Christ, Incarnate Word of God, *save us.*
Blood of Christ, of the New and
Eternal Testament, *save us.*
Blood of Christ, falling upon the earth
in the Agony, *save us.*
Blood of Christ, shed profusely in the Scourging, *save us.*
Blood of Christ, flowing forth
in the Crowning with Thorns, *save us.*
Blood of Christ, poured out on the Cross, *save us.*
Blood of Christ, price of our salvation, *save us.*
Blood of Christ, without which
there is no forgiveness, *save us.*
Blood of Christ, Eucharistic drink
and refreshment of souls, *save us.*
Blood of Christ, stream of mercy, *save us.*
Blood of Christ, victor over demons, *save us.*
Blood of Christ, courage of Martyrs, *save us.*
Blood of Christ, strength of Confessors, *save us.*
Blood of Christ, bringing forth Virgins, *save us.*

Blood of Christ, help of those in peril, *save us.*
Blood of Christ, relief of the burdened, *save us.*
Blood of Christ, solace in sorrow, *save us.*
Blood of Christ, hope of the penitent, *save us.*
Blood of Christ, consolation of the dying, *save us.*
Blood of Christ, peace and tenderness of hearts, *save us.*
Blood of Christ, pledge of eternal life, *save us.*
Blood of Christ, freeing souls from purgatory, *save us.*
Blood of Christ, most worthy of all glory
and honour, *save us.*

Lamb of God, who take away the sins of the world,
spare us, O Lord.
Lamb of God, who take away the sins of the world,
graciously hear us, O Lord.
Lamb of God, who take away the sins of the world,
have mercy on us.

V. You have redeemed us, O Lord, in your Blood.

R. And made us, for our God, a kingdom.

Let us pray.
Almighty and eternal God, you have appointed your only-begotten Son the Redeemer of the world, and willed to be appeased by his Blood. Grant we beg of you, that we may worthily adore this price of our salvation, and through its power be safeguarded from the evils of the present life, so that we may rejoice in its fruits forever in Heaven. Through the same Christ our Lord. Amen.

Litany of the Blessed Virgin Mary

Lord, have mercy.
Christ, have mercy.
Lord, have mercy.
Christ, hear us.
Christ, graciously hear us.

God, the Father of Heaven, *have mercy on us.*
God the Son, Redeemer of the world, *have mercy on us.*
God, the Holy Spirit, *have mercy on us.*
Holy Trinity, One God, *have mercy on us.*

Holy Mary, *pray for us.*
Holy Mother of God, *pray for us.*
Holy Virgin of virgins, *pray for us.*
Mother of Christ, *pray for us.*
Mother of divine grace, *pray for us.*
Mother most pure, *pray for us.*
Mother most chaste, *pray for us.*
Mother inviolate, *pray for us.*
Mother undefiled, *pray for us.*
Mother most amiable, *pray for us.*
Mother most admirable, *pray for us.*
Mother of good counsel, *pray for us.*
Mother of our Creator, *pray for us.*
Mother of our Saviour, *pray for us.*
Virgin most prudent, *pray for us.*
Virgin most venerable, *pray for us.*

Virgin most renowned, *pray for us.*
Virgin most powerful, *pray for us.*
Virgin most merciful, *pray for us.*
Virgin most faithful, *pray for us.*
Mirror of justice, *pray for us.*
Seat of wisdom, *pray for us.*
Cause of our joy, *pray for us.*
Spiritual vessel, *pray for us.*
Vessel of honour, *pray for us.*
Singular vessel of devotion, *pray for us.*
Mystical rose, *pray for us.*
Tower of David, *pray for us.*
Tower of ivory, *pray for us.*
House of gold, *pray for us.*
Ark of the covenant, *pray for us.*
Gate of Heaven, *pray for us.*
Morning star, *pray for us.*
Health of the sick, *pray for us.*
Refuge of sinners, *pray for us.*
Comforter of the afflicted, *pray for us.*
Help of Christians, *pray for us.*
Queen of angels, *pray for us.*
Queen of patriarchs, *pray for us.*
Queen of prophets, *pray for us.*
Queen of apostles, *pray for us.*
Queen of martyrs, *pray for us.*
Queen of confessors, *pray for us.*

Queen of virgins, *pray for us.*
Queen of all saints, *pray for us.*
Queen conceived without original sin, *pray for us.*
Queen assumed into Heaven, *pray for us.*
Queen of the most holy Rosary, *pray for us.*
Queen of peace, *pray for us.*

Lamb of God, who take away the sins of the world,
spare us, O Lord.
Lamb of God, who take away the sins of the world,
graciously hear us, O Lord.
Lamb of God, who take away the sins of the world,
have mercy on us, O Lord.

V. Pray for us O holy Mother of God.

R. That we may be made worthy of the promises of Christ.

Let us pray.
Grant unto us, your servants,
we beseech you, O Lord God,
at all times to enjoy health of soul and body;
and by the glorious intercession of Blessed Mary, ever Virgin,
when freed from the sorrows of this present life,
to enter into that joy which has no end.
We ask this through Christ our Lord.
Amen.

Litany of the Saints

Lord, have mercy.
Christ, have mercy.
Lord, have mercy.
Christ, hear us.
Christ, graciously hear us.

God, the Father of Heaven, *have mercy on us.*
God the Son, Redeemer of the world, *have mercy on us.*
God, the Holy Spirit, *have mercy on us.*
Holy Trinity, One God, *have mercy on us.*

Holy Mary, Mother of God, *pray for us.*
Ss Michael, Gabriel, and Raphael, *pray for us.*
All you holy Angels of God, *pray for us.*
St Elijah, *pray for us.*
St John the Baptist, *pray for us.*
St Joseph, *pray for us.*
All you holy Patriarchs and Prophets, *pray for us.*
Ss Peter and Paul, *pray for us.*
St Andrew, *pray for us.*
Ss John and James, *pray for us.*
All you holy Apostles and Evangelists, *pray for us.*
St Mary Magdalene, *pray for us.*
All you holy Disciples of the Lord, *pray for us.*
St Stephen, *pray for us.*
St Lawrence, *pray for us.*
Ss Perpetua and Felicity, *pray for us.*

All you holy Martyrs, *pray for us.*
St Gregory, *pray for us.*
St Ambrose, *pray for us.*
St Jerome, *pray for us.*
St Augustine, *pray for us.*
St Martin, *pray for us.*
St Anthony, *pray for us.*
St Benedict, *pray for us.*
Ss Francis and Dominic, *pray for us.*
Ss Ignatius of Loyola and Francis Xavier, *pray for us.*
St John Marie Vianney, *pray for us.*
St Catherine of Siena, *pray for us.*
St Teresa of Jesus, *pray for us.*
All you Saints of God, *pray for us.*

Be merciful, *deliver us, O Lord.*
From all evil, *deliver us, O Lord.*
From all sin, *deliver us, O Lord.*
From the snares of the Devil, *deliver us, O Lord.*
From everlasting death, *deliver us, O Lord.*
By your nativity, *deliver us, O Lord.*
By your baptism and holy fasting, *deliver us, O Lord.*
By your cross and passion, *deliver us, O Lord.*
By your death and burial, *deliver us, O Lord.*
By your holy resurrection, *deliver us, O Lord.*
By your wondrous ascension, *deliver us, O Lord.*

By the coming of the Holy Spirit, the Paraclete,
deliver us, O Lord.
On the day of judgment, *deliver us, O Lord.*

Christ, Son of the living God, *have mercy on us.*
You who for our sake were tempted by the Devil,
have mercy on us.
You who set free those beset by unclean spirits,
have mercy on us.
You who gave your disciples power over demons,
have mercy on us.
You who are seated at the right hand of the Father
and intercede for us,
have mercy on us.
You who will come to judge the living and the dead,
have mercy on us.

We are sinners, *we beseech you to hear us.*
That you would spare us, *we beseech you to hear us.*
That you would pardon us, *we beseech you to hear us.*
That you would strengthen and preserve us
in your holy service, *we beseech you to hear us.*
That you would raise up our minds to heavenly desires,
we beseech you to hear us.
That you would grant to your Church that she may serve
you in freedom and safety, *we beseech you to hear us.*

That you would bestow upon all peoples peace
and true concord, *we beseech you to hear us.*
That it may please you to hear us,
we beseech you to hear us.

Lamb of God, who take away the sins of the world,
spare us, O Lord.
Lamb of God, who take away the sins of the world,
graciously hear us, O Lord.
Lamb of God, who take away the sins of the world,
have mercy on us, O Lord.

V. Pray for us Holy Angels and Saints of God.

R. That we may be made worthy of the promises
of Christ.

Let us pray.
O God, whose nature it is always to have mercy
and to spare your people:
receive our supplication,
and grant that your servants,
whom the Devil has bound with the chains of his power,
may be freed by your mercy and loving kindness.
We ask this through Christ our Lord.
Amen.

Spiritual Warfare

Fighting the Good Fight

Every Christian is engaged in an ongoing struggle against the self, and against temptation, striving to gain the blessings of the Kingdom of God. This booklet enlightens the struggle by searching the wisdom of the scriptures. It gives hope to everyone, because Christ is always by our side to help us in every battle, and he has already defeated death and sin.

ISBN: 978 1 86082 421 0
CTS Code: SP16

Exorcism

Understanding exorcism in scripture and practice

Both secularism and superstition have popularised some very distorted ideas about exorcism. This booklet, written by an experienced exorcist, looks at its origin in the Gospels and its practice in the Church today. Different kinds of demonic influence are discussed, including their relation to conversion and sin and mental illness. Above all the text gives the good news that in Christ the Devil is already defeated and that the Church carries this victory to those in need.

ISBN: 978 1 86082 502 6
CTS Code: Ex27

Catholic Prayer Book

A book of basic prayers from a range of sources

The raising of the heart and mind to God'. This traditional definition of prayer sums up what should be a regular activity for all of us. As we say at every Mass 'It is right to give him thanks and praise'. Prayer is, first of all, acknowledging God's call and responding to Him in humility. As the Catechism of the Catholic Church states in a wonderful quote from St Thérèse of Lisieux: For me, prayer is a surge of the heart; it is a simple look turned toward heaven, it is a cry of recognition and of love, embracing both trial and joy, (*CCC* 2558).

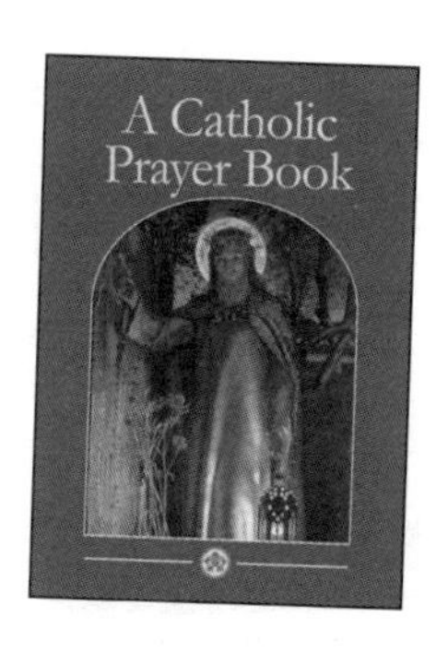

ISBN: 978 1 86082 089 2
CTS Code: D582